PUFFIN BOOKS

Editor: Kaye Webb

The Big Book of Puzzles

One day, when he was nine-years old, Karl Friedrich Gauss solved a puzzle. It wasn't an easy puzzle: his teacher told the class to add together all the numbers from one to one hundred and Karl Friedrich wrote the answer down straight away!

Could you do that? You can if you read this book, and Karl Friedrich Gauss grew up to become one of the world's greatest mathematicians and physicists! But there are lots more puzzles in this fascinating collection for you to solve. There are riddles to answer; tricks to try out on your friends and family; optical illusions galore; and games to play. There is something here for everyone, whether you like playing with numbers, thinking up words, working out secret codes – or just puzzling over pictures. (And you can always amaze people by adding up those numbers one to one hundred in double-quick time!)

The Big Book of Puzzles

By Michael Holt and Ronald Ridout

Illustrated by Peter Edwards

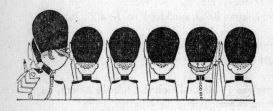

PUFFIN BOOKS

Puffin Books,
Penguin Books Ltd,
Harmondsworth, Middlesex, England
Penguin Books Australia Ltd,
Ringwood, Victoria, Australia
Penguin Books Canada Ltd,
41 Steelcase Road West, Markham, Ontario, Canada
Penguin Books (N.Z.) Ltd,
182–190 Wairau Road, Auckland 10, New Zealand

First published by Longman Young Books 1972
Published in Puffin Books 1976

Made and printed in Great Britain by
Cox & Wyman Ltd, London, Reading and Fakenham
Set in Monotype Joanna

To our children –

and especially to Miranda
who invented the new kind
of crossword on page 67.

Hints on How to Use this Book

In this book you will find a great many puzzles of various kinds. Many are brand new, one or two have never seen the inside of a book before, and we couldn't resist including some old chestnuts, with a new twist of course. In fact there is something for all the family.

There are two main types of puzzles here – word puzzles and maths brain-teasers. The word puzzles include anagrams, acrostics, crosswords (both usual and of a new sort we invented), hidden words in sentences, spelling bees, word meanings and dictionary tests. The maths ones cover number tricks, magic squares, paper cutting, reasoning maps (again, specially devised for this book), and trick questions to try on your friends!

When you see [turtle] next to a puzzle, you can be sure it's an easy one. So you can always warm up on one of these but don't spend too long on it if you can't see the catch.

If you see this sign [pointing hand] then you'd better watch out for a brain-teaser. The puzzle may not be as simple as it looks. Or it may be a tricky catch question. If you don't see the catch, leave it and try an easy puzzle to give you confidence. Then come back to the brain-teaser when you feel up to it.

You'll find the answers starting on page 113 at the back of the book.

We hope you have fun!

MH
RR

Seeing is believing

Is it really a spiral? Seeing is believing, they say. Actually it's a series of circles within circles! You can check this by tracing round with your finger. You'll find lots more of these 'Seeing-is-believing' pictures throughout this book.

1 . Set Arthur free

The star marks the Star Chamber in the castle where young
Arthur is lost. The marked path shows one way he can get out
by moving only through even-numbered rooms.

Can you find another way out – using only even numbers
divisible by three?

For example, 12 is even and it is divisible by 3 because
12 ÷ 3 = 4.

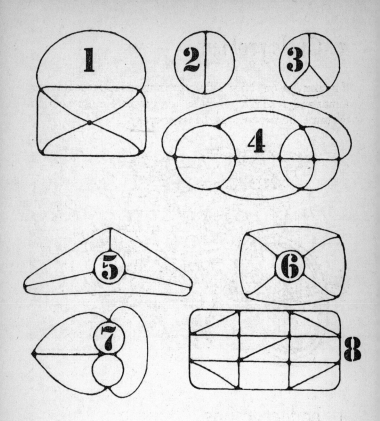

2. One-stroke curves

How many of these curves can you copy in one stroke without lifting your pencil and without going over the same line twice?

3. Cycle problem

If it takes Sue one hour and twenty minutes to bicycle to her
Aunt's and it takes her brother David seventy minutes to do
the same journey, who is the faster cycler?

4. Laddergraphs

Notice how you can change MICE into CATS in four moves,
changing only one letter at a time and always making a complete word:

```
M   I   C   E
M   A   C   E
M   A   T   E
M   A   T   S
C   A   T   S
```

This is called a *laddergraph*.

1. Now turn DUST into TANK in four steps, changing one letter at a time.
   These clues may help you:
   DUST
   . . . .   Evening
   . . . .   An elephant has two
   . . . .   A job of work
   TANK

2. Now turn LANE into POST:
   LANE
   . . . .   The only one
   . . . .   Miss
   . . . .   Not found
   POST

3. Turn BASK into DIRT:
   BASK
   . . . .   Outside of tree
   . . . .   Not light
   . . . .   For throwing
   DIRT

4. Turn, if you can, BACK into LINE:
   BACK
   . . . .   Place to keep money in
   . . . .   Ruin of your life
   . . . .   Country road
   LINE

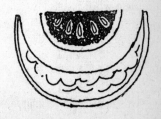

5. Analogies

Can you complete these analogies, as they are called? The first one is done for you.

1. Melon is to rind
   as animal is to — body head *skin* blood   Answer: *skin*
2. Up is to down as
   left is to —   front back side right
3. Few is to many
   as less is to —   several more big fewer
4. Height is to tall
   as width is to —   wide fat round thin
5. Dog is to fur as
   bird is to —   skin down feathers quill
6. Ship is to water
   as aeroplane is
   to —   waves air flight cloud
7. Hat is to head as
   lid is to —   box cup table bottle
8. House is to roof
   as head is to —   top tile hair neck
9. Few is to many
   as seldom is
   to —   several often rarely more
10. Wall is to brick
    as skeleton is
    to —   skull legs bone flesh

Here's your rating:
10 Excellent
9 Very good
8 Good
7 Fair
6 or less – Brush-up needed!

6. Matching pairs

By linking the words in the first column to the right ones from the second column, you can make twenty pairs that are in common use. The first pair is KNIFE and FORK. See how quickly you can form all pairs. Here is your rating:

20	Great!
17	Very good
15	Good
12	Fair
11 or less	} Mmmm!

1. knife			dog
2. spoon			vinegar
3. cat			cheese
4. oil			cart
5. chalk			bolt
6. house			braces
7. horse			pusher
8. belt			garden
9. nut			shovel
10. pick	*and*		fork
11. spit			sound
12. neat			drum
13. bib			day
14. fife			tidy
15. king			spice
16. night			low
17. sugar			white
18. safe			queen
19. black			tucker
20. high			polish

7. Riddle

Why did the lobster blush?

8. Highhat or broadbrim ?

Which do you think is longer — the full width of the brim of the man's hat or its height?

Guess before you measure the two lengths.

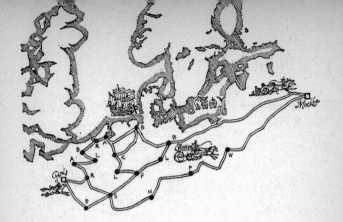

9. An odd trip

Can you drive from Paris to Moscow and pass through an
even number of cities? Each dot is a city and only one is the
key to the correct route. Don't count PARIS or MOSCOW.

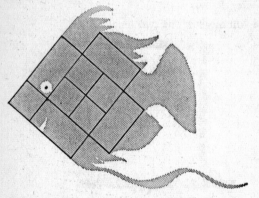

10. Fishy squares

How many different squares can you find in this picture?
There may be more than you can see at first glance.

11. Matching words

How quickly can you find the other member of the pair?
The first pair is OVER and ABOVE.

1. over and	square
2. fair and	dry
3. high and	above
4. ways and	nail
5. brace and	ashes
6. pots and	bit
7. safe and	means
8. part and	pans
9. tooth and	parcel
10. stocks and	socket
11. ball and	ruin
12. goods and	sound
13. sackcloth and	chattels
14. rack and	baggage
15. bag and	shares

1 2. New Year Birthday Honours

What animal has the same official birthday, 1 January, whenever it is born?

1 3. Matching socks

Fiona was going to a party. Just as she was about to open a drawerful of socks, the upstairs lights fused. She had to find a matching pair of socks in the dark. How few need she take downstairs into the light to be sure of getting a matching pair? (She only has two kinds!)

Here's the drawerful of socks – by daylight!

14. Word-delving

You have to delve in the DICTIONARY to find these words. The words required by the clues can all be formed from the letters of the one word DICTIONARY. Can you find them?

1. To mend by passing thread in and out in two directions. Answer: *darn*
2. Something given in the change.
3. Movement.
4. A daily record of events.
5. A place where milk is kept and butter made.
6. Slightly less than a metre.
7. A fixed allowance.
8. To move forward suddenly and quickly.
9. The choice and use of the spoken word.
10. Saying something which is the opposite of what one really thinks, in order to make a point.

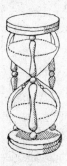

15. Upside-down

What date within the last hundred years reads the same upside-down?

16. Tiny Tim's joke

The Cratchetts had such a Christmas spread that there was more than enough food for all six Cratchetts. When it came to the tangerines, Tiny Tim didn't want one. And Mrs Cratchett had given out five tangerines each. So Tiny Tim, who had learnt the new maths, switched the fruit round like this:

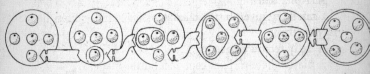

Can you write the bits of the multiplication tables that his practical joke obeys?

17. Before your very eyes

How many true circles are there here?

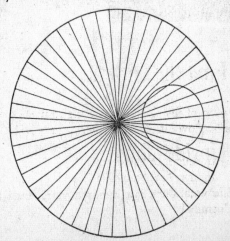

18. Brainwave's eggsample

Professor Brainwave found these seven dinosaur eggs in a square field. He wanted to fence them off from each other – in case they hatched, he said – with three straight fences only.

His assistant tried this:

'Done!' he cried.

'No – that's four fences,' the Professor said.

'It can be done with three fences, only I've forgotten how just now!'

Can you do it for the Professor?

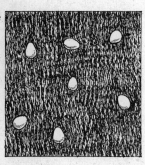
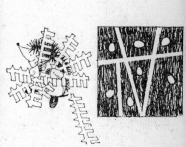

19. Find the vowels

With the aid of the clues, add vowels to make these letters into words. How quickly can you do them all? The first is OHIO.

H	an American state
DH	another American state
Z	animal garden
GRLL	animal

RB	breed of horse
PR	musical play
CRB	Canadian reindeer
MPRR	a ruler
S	a continent
RP	another continent
W	animal (four legs)
B	insect (six legs)
B	reptile (no legs)
P	animal (2 legs)
B	musical instrument
K	a tree
R	a country
NN	a vegetable
Y	part of the head
SS	desert watering place

20. Magic square

This square is magic! Add all the rows, and the columns, like this:

$16 + 2 + 3 + 13 = ?$
$16 + 5 + 9 + 4 \quad = ?$ and so on.

What do you see that is rather magical?

Now add the two diagonals:

$\qquad 16 + 11 + 6 + 1 = ?$
$\qquad$ and $13 + 10 + 7 + 4 = ?$

16	2	3	13
5	11	10	8
9	7	6	12
4	14	15	1

Having done that, add the middle four numbers.
  What do you find?
  Add up the corner blocks of four – like $16 + 2 + 5 + 11$, in the top left corner, and what do you find again?

Now swop the two middle columns, as shown by the arrows.
  Work out the same sums again.
  Is the square still magic?

21. Concatenations !

This lovely word means joining up bits of words. For example, you can place the syllable un- in front of these syllables – simply think of 'un' printed inside each box here:

☐ done ☐ tied ☐ made

What syllable could you put in each box – the same syllable – to fit all the word endings given?

1. ☐ sist
   ☐ tain
   ☐ ifer
   ☐ tinue

2. ☐ clude
   ☐ capable
   ☐ dicate
   ☐ finite

3. ☐ pendicular
   ☐ petual
   ☐ sist
   ☐ fume

4. ☐ fine
   ☐ feat
   ☐ mand
   ☐ prive

5. ☐ mit
   ☐ just
   ☐ vance
   ☐ vise

6. ☐ fog
   ☐ head
   ☐ hind
   ☐ lieve

7. ☐ miss
   ☐ ease
   ☐ cuss
   ☐ cover

8. ☐ iverse
   ☐ less
   ☐ til
   ☐ it

9. ☐ long
   ☐ low
   ☐ neath
   ☐ ing

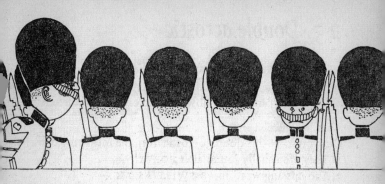

22. As you were

The new Sergeant gave these orders to his squad:
'Right turn! Left turn!
Left turn! Left turn! Right turn!'

Sam Smart, one of the soldiers, simply turned left.

Was he facing the way he should have been – that is, the same way as the rest of the squad finished up?

23. Next please !

What number comes next?

1, 2, 4, 7, 11, 16, □

24. Simple sum

Take one from nine and leave ten!

25. Double acrostic

Here is an example of a double acrostic. Notice that in addition to the words you can read across, the initial letters of the words can be read down and so can the final letters of the words.

Can you solve this double acrostic from the following clues?
1. They are usually found after FORTY.
2. The missing word in AS SWIFT AS AN —.
3. Pigs used to be called this.
4. Commerce.
5. Anyone can be wise after this.

Initial letters: The missing word in ' — not, want not'.
Final letters: The proverb says 'a rose by any other name would smell as — '.

1	H	E	A	R	T
2	A	P	A	C	E
3	S	A	U	C	E
4	T	I	G	H	T
5	E	A	R	T	H

1					
2					
3					
4					
5					

26. More concatenations

Here's a slightly different way of stringing bits of words together.

What you have to do is to find the single same word-ending to fit on to all these beginnings.

For example, -tain fits all these strings:

con ☐
de ☐
abs ☐
per ☐

See if you can do these:

1. con ☐	2. abs ☐	3. pre ☐
de ☐	con ☐	con ☐
in ☐	de ☐	de ☐
per ☐	re ☐	re ☐

27. Berlin–Paris Express

Help Colonel Blankety-Blank find the fastest route from Berlin to Paris. Trains stop at every station, shown by letters. So the fastest route passes through the fewest stations. Bridges don't count as stations, of course.

means a bridge.

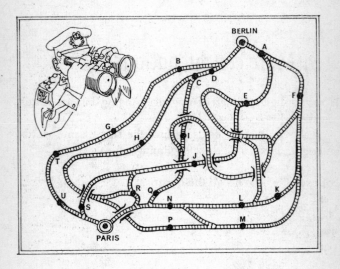

28. Reverse it

$23 + 9 = 32$

See how the digits of twenty-three are reversed when you add nine.

What other two-figure numbers can you add nine to and reverse their digits?

29. Act on these clues

The words you have to find from these clues all end with ACT. The first, for example, is DISTRACT. How quickly can you find the others?

1. The act which draws the attention away.
2. The act which gets your attention.
3. The act which is accurate.
4. The act which takes away.
5. The act which takes things out.
6. The act which is closely packed together.
7. The act which makes an agreement.
8. The act which means a collision.
9. The act which shows respect for people's feelings.
10. The act which carries out business.

30. In the balance

From the pictures, can you tell how many marbles will balance the box?

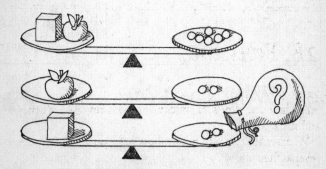

31. What's next?

O, T, T, F, F, S, S, . . .

Hint: it's not very mathematical!

32. Scrambled snap-shots

Put these pictures in the order they must have happened:

33. What's next?

1, 1, 2, 3, 5, 8, 13, ☐

Clue: $2 = 1 + 1$, $3 = 2 + 1$

34. Spiral crossword

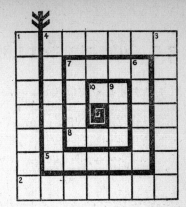

Here are the clues to this spiral crossword.

Can you solve it?

Follow the direction of the arrow round the spiral to find the start of the next clue.

Make sure to copy the spiral on to a sheet of paper – unless, of course, the book is yours – before doing it.

Across

2. To find the length of.
4. Icecream with fruit.
5. A stick for a post, that rhymes with break.
7. A young sheep.
8. You see with this.
10. Short for company.

Down

1. Dull and commonplace; it begins by singing with closed lips.
3. To shut out; it rhymes with mood.
4. Pressure; it rhymes with dress.
6. You do this to stop in a car.
7. Unable to walk normally, through injury.
9. The first whole number.

35. The English Family Robinson

This is the Robinson's family 'tree', drawn with arrows. Each arrow means 'has as a brother'.

Can you tell who is a man and who is a woman?

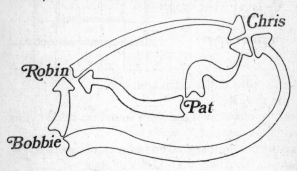

36. Quickie

Can you build a house with its four walls all facing north?

37. A striking puzzle

A clock strikes six in five seconds.
How long does it take it to strike twelve?

38. Take your partners

By adding to the words in the first column the right ones from the second column, you can make twenty pairs that are in everyday use. The first pair is BROKEN PROMISES.

See how quickly you can form all twenty pairs.

Here is your rating:

1 min.	Excellent
2 min.	Very good
3 min.	Good
4 min.	Fair
5 min.	Try again

1.	broken	tooth
2.	flat	wet
3.	common	gale
4.	food	tyre
5.	sweet	mechanic
6.	Yorkshire	sense
7.	summer	poisoning
8.	garage	grease
9.	blind	holiday
10.	elbow	Tom
11.	Catherine	drunk
12.	mother	promises
13.	soaking	wheels
14.	peeping	pudding
15.	Brazil	corner
16.	plain	tongue
17.	howling	nuts
18.	topsy	Jane
19.	tight	enterprise
20.	free	turvy

39. MIRROR ЯOЯЯIM

Barbra and Timothy went to a party. Everyone had their name, vertically, on a large card. When they stood in front of a mirror, they noticed a strange thing. Hold a mirror up to their names. Can you see what they found? Can you explain it?

40. The second man

Can you find the remaining person? In the first one, for example, if you remove the letters of the word MARINER, the word PARSON remains. See how quickly you can find the other remaining persons.

1. MAPRARISONERN
   Remove the seaman and a churchman remains.
2. BABKUTECHRER
   Remove the bread man and a meat man remains.

3. A R S E T P R O O N R A T U E R T
Remove the newspaper man and a spaceman remains.

4. P W A I R R L I O O T R
Remove the flying man and a fighting man remains.

5. L B A A W N D Y E I T R
Remove the man of law and a lawless man remains.

6. F T Y L O P I R S I S T T
Remove the writing girl and a flower girl remains.

7. S K U B I J N E C G T
Remove the ruling man and the ruled man remains.

8. A A R U T T I S H O R T
Remove the painting man and the writing man remains.

9. G P L L A U Z M I B E E R R
Remove the tap man and the glass man remains.

10. N U M R A T S R E O N
Remove the senior woman and the junior woman remains.

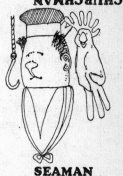

CHURCHMAN

SEAMAN

41. Bucket and spade

A plastic bucket and spade cost thirty pence together.

If the bucket cost ten pence more than the spade, how much did the spade cost?

Maths made easy!

Lewis Carroll wrote the *Alice* books. His best kind of maths was the sort where somebody else does the work!

Here's how:

Pick a date you know (1066, say). Add 10000.

Subtract 1.

Jot the result on a scrap of paper. Fold it and hand it to a friend to keep.

Now say to him:
  When was the Battle of Hastings?
  Write it down.   1066
  Now write any four figures under that.'

He writes (say):   7201
Now you pretend to scribble any four numbers
under that: 2798
                                                          ─────────
  (Actually, each number you write adds up   11065
with his number to make 9. $7 + 2 = 9$, and so
on.)

You say:
'Add up the numbers. The answer is on the scrap of paper!'

Does it always work?

42. April Fool ?

How many months have twenty-eight days?

43. Frog-in-well

A frog at the bottom of a well ten metres deep, begins to climb out. He climbs up three metres every day but slips back two metres each night.

After how many days will he be free?

44. Quizzle

What word is always pronounced wrongly?

Amaze with a maze!

Get a friend to draw you a single closed maze on a large sheet of paper. Tell him to cover the edges quickly with newspaper, leaving an oblong of the maze uncovered.

Now mark several spots on the uncovered maze. You tell him: 'When you remove the papers, all my marks will be found to be inside the maze.' When your friend does so, he will find you are right.

How is it done?

The secret is, note one spot that is inside the maze as he is laying the newspapers round the edge of the maze (like our X).

Mark that first. Now, how can you work out whether any other bit of the maze is inside or outside?

When you are practising, put your finger on the chosen spot *inside* the maze. Run it over the maze. Cross one wall and you are outside. Cross another wall and you are inside again. And so on. The rule is: Cross an even number of walls and you are still inside the maze. Cross an odd number and you are outside.

45. Word square

Here is a word square completed for you. Word squares are really crossword puzzles that are absolutely square. Not only does the completed puzzle read across and down, but it produces the same words each way and in the same order.

How quickly can you solve this word square? There are two sets of clues to help you.

Across
1. An alcoholic drink.
2. A notion.
3. Close.
4. To deserve.

Down
1. A drink made from grapes.
2. A picture in the mind.
3. Not distant.
4. To get in return for work.

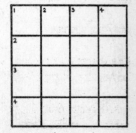

46. Parallel lines?

Railway lines or a ladder? The top rung is longer than the lower one – or is it?

    Try turning the book. Does it make any difference?

47. Riddle

Why couldn't the viper vipe her nose

The Missing Slice

Where has the missing slice of pie gone?
  Just turn the picture upside-down and you'll see!

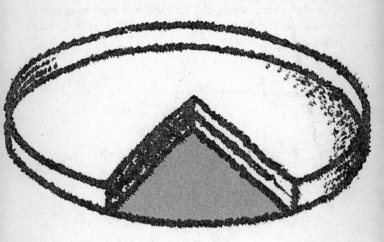

48. Words that count

Can you say what these odd words are about?

ane	sother	een dick	een bumfrey
tane	lother	teen dick	teen bumfrey
tother	co	tother dick	tother bumfrey
feather	deffrey	feather dick	feather bumfrey
flip	dick	bumfrey	gigit

49. Gromek, very much !

In Slobodia, they only have two coins, a Slob which is like a penny and a Gromek. The Gromek is worth two Slob.

How many different ways can you pay for a bag of Slobodian sweets worth five Slob without needing change?

For instance, you could pay two Gromek, one Slob: that's one way.

50. Glidogram

The clues to this glidogram are:

1. Sham; not genuine.
2. The form of a globe.
3. A fever that is accompanied by purple spots on the body.
4. Some of the lesser Greek goddesses; now any beautiful young women.

5. A title once used by rulers descended from Mohammed.
6. Prize for winning a tournament.
7. A bottle from which soda water can be forced out by the pressure of the gas in it.
8. A very enigmatic figure from Egypt.
9. A group of words belonging together.

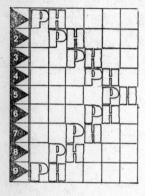

5 1 . The sign

What do you think this sign says?
   'Paris in the Spring'?
   Read it again then.

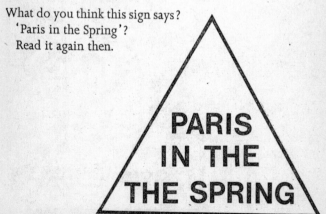

52. Mirror writing

One day in a boring maths lesson, Sue wanted to ask her friend Sally if teacher's pet, Jennie, was top of the class again. So she wrote her a note:

$$907\ 314436\ 21$$

Can you read the message? Use a mirror and read backwards.

Sally wrote back:

$9 + 0 + 7 + 3 + 1 + 4 + 4 + 3 + 6 + 2 + 1 =$

Do the sum to find the answer.

The teacher found the notes but instead of being angry with the girls, she praised them, of course, for doing sums!

53. Picture puzzle

Can you pair the picture clues to make four bigger words?

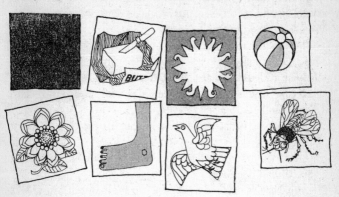

54. Seating problems

Six children, Ann, Bob, Chris, Dina, Ed, Fred, are sitting at a round table. Ann is two along from Dina, who is sitting next to Fred, on his left. Also two along from Dina sits Bob, next to whom is Chris. Ann exclaims: 'Super! I've got Chris on one side and Ed on the other.'

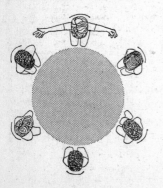

Can you show how they are seated at the table?

55. Punctuation puzzles

Can you punctuate each sentence below – put in full stops, commas, and so on – so that it makes sense?
We have done the first for you.

1. The landlord of the 'Horse and Cart' pub wrote a cross note to his signwriter: 'There is too much space between Horse and and and and and Cart. This should read: 'There is too much space between 'Horse' and 'and' and 'and' and 'Cart'.'

2. that that is is that that is not is not that that is not is not that that is

3. Jones had had had had had had been in Smith's essay Smith had been top

4. King Charles cracked a joke half an hour after his head was cut off

5. a window cleaner was busy cleaning traffic from inside the car didn't sound too loud cried the Major taxi inside a nearby telephone kiosk a lollipop in one hand and a plastic gun in the other sticking his tongue out at the motorists a small boy hung about while his aunt telephoned the Major a cab

56. Corking good puzzle

A bottle and a cork cost three pence.
  The bottle costs one penny more than the cork.
  How much does each cost?

57. When is a square not a square?

Answer: When it doesn't look like one!

Which of these shapes do you think is a perfect square?

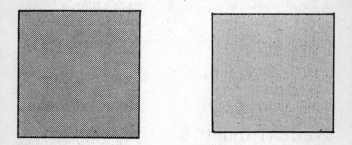

Which of these squares is the larger?

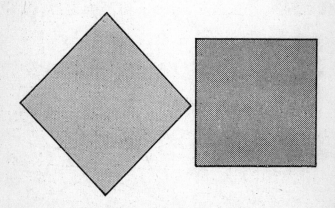

58. Word-making

You all know the pencil and paper game where you are given a longish word and have to see how many shorter words you can make from it. This puzzle is a variation of that game. You have to make certain words from NEWSPAPER, using the clues below. The first word is SEEP.

1. To ooze out.
2. To use bad language.
3. A quick secretive look.
4. A tree fruit.
5. Close.
6. A seat in a church.
7. To use a needle.
8. The glass in a window.
9. A very small bird.
10. The back of the neck.

Number magic !

First, add up the numbers

across ↔
down ↕
and slant-wise, this way ↗
and that way: ↘
   What do you notice?

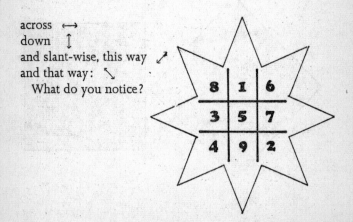

Here's a trick you can play on a friend. Find a book. Open it at page fifteen. Pick the 1st word on the 5th line. Write it down on a slip of paper. Fold the paper and ask your friend to put it in his pocket, unseen.

Give him this magic square. Tell him: add up any row, column, or slant line. That done, hand him your book. Tell him: look up the page given by the result; find the line given by the second figure (5) and the word given by the first figure (1); compare with the slip of paper. He will find you are able to read his mind!

ABC of verbs

How quickly can you write down a list of action words (verbs) in A B C order? 'To X-ray' is allowed for X.

You can begin like this: *Act, Barge, Catch* ... Rate yourself like this:

1 minute	Remarkable
2 minutes	Excellent
3 minutes	Good
4 minutes	Promising
5 minutes	More practice needed
8 minutes	Not your day!

59. Riddle

There were millions of people in London yesterday. Why?

Think of a number

Think of a number, from 1 to 9.
Multiply the result by 5.
Add 3.
Double the result.
And you have a 2-figure number ending in a 6. Strike that off.
And you have the number you first thought of!
Girl: I've thought of 3.
I multiply it by 5: that makes 15.
I add 3: that makes 18.
I double that: 36.
Knock off the 6. Yes!
I've got the number I first thought of, 3.
Try it on your friends.
It always works.

60. Four-in-a-row

Four children are sitting in a row. Bob is sitting next to Charles and on his left. Doris sits immediately on Charles' right. Ann sits somewhere to the left of Doris. (She doesn't have to be next to her.)

Put the children in order.

61 . Sum puzzle

As early as nine years old, Karl Friedrich Gauss showed how clever he was at mathematics. He went on to become one of the world's greatest mathematicians.

His teacher asked the class to add all the numbers from one to a hundred. No sooner had the teacher written the problem on the board than the young Gauss wrote the correct answer on his slate.

You can see how he probably worked it out from this simpler sum.

How do you add all the numbers 1, 2, 3, 4, 5?

First make a wall or draw one like this:

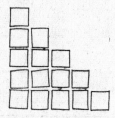

Then do the same again,
upside down:

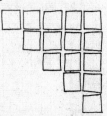

Put the walls together to make an oblong.

Can you tell what the sum 1 + 2 + 3 + 4 + 5 is now?
How do you add the numbers from 1 to 6 in this way?

62. Word strips

Here is another kind of crossword puzzle.

This is how it goes. The clues tell you what the letters are and you have to work out where they go.

Suppose the word is SOLVE. Check the clues against the filled-in word strip here.

Clues

The letter O comes before L.

V is before E and after L.

S is three squares above V.

You should be able to solve it from that.

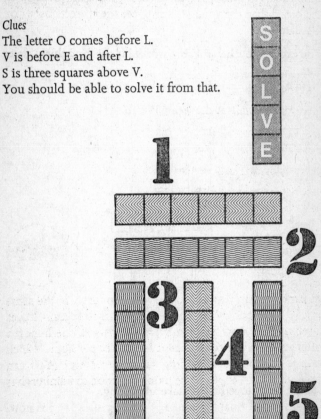

Now try these word strips:

1. The letter U is on the immediate left of M.
   N is next to U.
   R is on the far right of M.
   And E is before R and after B.

2. M is on the immediate right of A.
   P is right of M and left of E.
   D is immediately left of A and far left of R, which is right of E.

3. T is exactly in the middle.
   A comes before E.
   W comes before T and E.
   R is three squares below A.

4. T is two letters above E.
   S comes before O and N.
   E is immediately after N.

5. B comes before O and R.
   R comes after X and E.
   E is two squares after O.

63. Express sum

An express train leaves London for Edinburgh at the same time – 2 o'clock in the afternoon – as a slow train leaves Edinburgh for London. The express travels at one hundred miles an hour, the slow train at fifty miles per hour. Which train is farther from London when they meet? (You can forget about the length of the trains.) London to Edinburgh is four hundred miles.

Clue: Don't spend *too* long over it!

64. April Fool joke

If I have fifty pigs and take away all but five, how many do I
have left?

LEAVE NO
LITTER

65. How many squares?

How many squares can you find on this board?

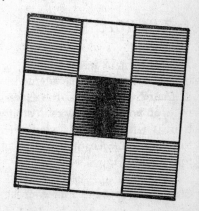

66. Loony limericks

Here is a limerick written by the poet Edward Lear:

> There was a Young Lady of Welling,
> Whose praise all the world was a-telling;
>   She played on the harp,
>   And caught several Carp,
> That accomplished Young Lady of Welling.

You get the pattern of lines and rhymes, don't you? See how quickly you can unscramble the following limericks – some by Lear – in which the lines have got in the wrong order.

Put the lines in their proper order again.

Here is your rating:

> 2 minutes: Super
> $2\frac{1}{2}$ minutes: Very good
> 3 minutes: Good
> $3\frac{1}{2}$ minutes: Fair
> 4 minutes: Have another try

1. Who said, 'If you choose to suppose
   That my nose is too long,
   You are certainly wrong!'
   There was an Old Man with a nose,
   That remarkable Man with a nose.

2. Inside the lamented
   There was a young lady of Ryde,
   The apples fermented
   And made cider inside her inside.
   Who ate green apples and died;

3. And sent to their Pa at Marseilles.
   There was an Old Man of Marseilles,
   They caught several fish,
   Whose daughters wore bottle-green veils;
   Which they put in a dish,

67. Cook to taste

Can you make this sum correct?

1 2 3 4 5 6 7 8 9 = 100

Use any of the signs +, —, ×, ÷ between the numbers on the left.

68. Letter-shuffling

Re-arrange the letters of the words on the left to make another word. The clues help.

END   (Place where lions live) Answer: DEN
FELT   (Not right)
SHORE   (You ride it)
SEAT   (Compass direction)
PEACH   (Not dear)
TAME   (It plays football)
PEST   (Gives you a rise)
TRACE   (Box)
FATE   (A deed)
DEAR   (What you do with a book)
WERE   (Jug)

69. Topsy-turvy years

Turn the year 1961 upside down and it looks the same. (Turn the book round and see!)

When was the last topsy-turvy year before 1961?

70. Riddle

When is a cube not a cube?

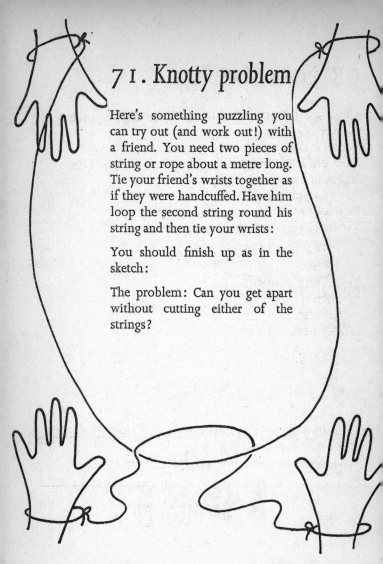

71. Knotty problem

Here's something puzzling you can try out (and work out!) with a friend. You need two pieces of string or rope about a metre long. Tie your friend's wrists together as if they were handcuffed. Have him loop the second string round his string and then tie your wrists:

You should finish up as in the sketch:

The problem: Can you get apart without cutting either of the strings?

72. Riddle

How many jelly-beans can you put in an empty jar?

73. Story pairs

Can you pair these story-book names properly?

Hansel and Tweedledum
Peter and Maid Marian
Robin Hood and the Wolf
Jack and Gretel
Tweedledee and Jill
The Mad Hatter and the March Hare

Bending the rule

Is this ruler really bent?

You'd better check with a ruler and see.

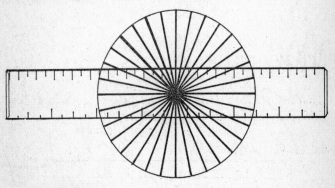

74. Riddle

When should you give a baby hippopotamus's milk?

75. Letter removal

Can you, by removing the right number of letters, produce the word required? The remaining letters must spell the word without changing their order in any way. The first word, for example, is EASE.

1. Take three letters from MEASURE to give freedom from discomfort.
2. Take two letters from APPLIED to make a fruit.
3. Take three letters from PILLOW to make you sick.
4. Take two letters from PLANET to make a narrow road.
5. Take three letters from STRANGER to spell mild wrath.
6. Take two letters from CHEDDAR to make a tree.
7. Take four letters from PROVIDE to make a pastry dish.
8. Take three letters from CABINET to make a kind of stick.
9. Take four letters from SKIPPING to make a ruler.
10. Take five letters from TEMPERATURE to make it ripe.

Screwy picture ?

Can the three nuts screw on to the three-pronged fork? Just how many prongs are there anyway?

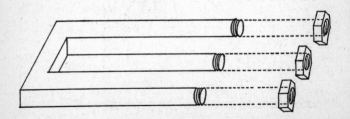

76. BAffling crossword

These are the clues to words that all begin with BA.
The squares indicate the number of letters in each word.
How quickly can you find all ten?

1. To make sounds like a baby.
2. An unmarried man.
3. The opposite of forward.
4. To puzzle completely.
5. Having little or no hair.
6. To give a vote.
7. With legs curving out at knees.
8. A formal feast.
9. Male voice between tenor and bass.
10. Shy.

1	B	A					
2	B	A					
3	B	A					
4	B	A					
5	B	A					
6	B	A					
7	B	A					
8	B	A					
9	B	A					
10	B	A					

77. Riddle

When is a door not a door?

78. Quick change

Each of these words can be turned into an entirely different word by merely changing one letter. See how quickly you can change all ten. The first one becomes MOANING.

1. Make MORNING feel sorry for itself.
2. Make TRUNK very unsteady.
3. Make STARCH look for something.
4. Make CHASM much more attractive.
5. Make ROUGH go with a cold.
6. Make LILY go with a swing.
7. Make THOUGH suitable for pigs.
8. Make PETROL see that all is well.
9. Give MASTERLY more direction.
10. Make WHISPER weak and frightened.

79. Inside-out sentences

What does this mean?
The Moon that the spaceman that we saw photographed whizzes through space.

Well, we can rewrite it like this:
We saw the spaceman that photographed the Moon that whizzes through space.

Can you say what these sentences mean?
1. The fiddles that the fiddlers three that the King praised brought that made the Queen laugh.
2. The team that the Martians that we cheered played brought a Martian goat for a mascot.
3. Speed that a wing that the humming-bird has is very fast.
4. The house that the malt that the rat that the cat that the dog that the cow with the crumpled horn tossed worried killed ate lay in Jack built.

80. Pocket-size coin

Can you put a penny on this table, placing it flat so it won't stick out over the edge?

Guess first, then try and see!

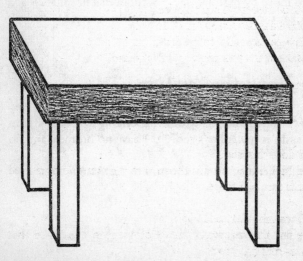

81. Back-to-front words

Some words when read backwards produce another word. For example, the word SPOT when read backwards gives us TOPS. Here are the clues to some more words like this. You can check your answer to the clue on the left, because the word when spelt backwards will give you the answer to the clue on the right. Thus the first two words are LIVE and EVIL.

WHEN READ FORWARDS	WHEN READ BACKWARDS
1. To exist.	Wicked.
2. To run liquidly.	A wild animal.
3. A heavenly body.	Rodents.
4. To cut with scissors.	Tiny wire pegs.
5. Portions.	A leather fastener.
6. Wild open land.	A space for living in.
7. A reel.	Curves crossing themselves.
8. Coarse water grass.	A speedy animal.
9. To move by pulling.	A room in a hospital.
10. A bar turned on a fulcrum.	To make merry.

82. Find the relation

'This person's father,' said the man pointing to a snap-shot in his hand, 'is my father's son. Yet I have no brothers and no sons.'

Well, what relation was the man to the man in the snap?

83. Spy codes

1. WILLY VAN TRUBCODE, the famous spy, found this message at his hotel. Luckily he knew that his name must be in it. Can you help him crack the code?

This is how Willy started. TRUBCODE has eight letters. There is only one word in the message of eight letters. So he wrote TRUBCODE beneath it and filled in all the other places where those letters appear. You carry on. Remember there is the rest of his name in the message.

2. Here's a message from JOHNNY BREAKFAST:

FH IM CBMHP FE MCH BIJ MGHH LBBD IKMHG MHD
FH GHINE MB MIJH MCH MGHILOGH ZBCDDE
FGHIJKILM.

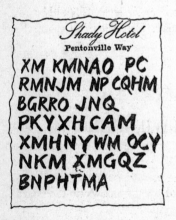

84. Letter plate or number plate

When Mr Lion bought a new car, he chose this old jalopy — because he wanted the number plate. 'It's really great!' he said.

Why do you think he liked it?

85. Tracking down animals

Here's a new kind of crossword.

In each clue, begin at and follow the arrows on the board in the directions shown by the clues.

1. The first is done for you. Can you find the names of three animals?

CLUES

The pictures are clues.

○⊙↑□↑□→□↑□

○→↑□↑□→↑□→□

○→↑□→□→□↑□↑□←□

○↑□→□→↑□↑□→□

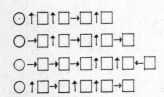

───────────────

○↑□↑□↑→□↑□

○→↑□↑□→□→□↑□

○↑□→□↑□→□→□↓□↓□

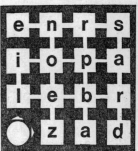

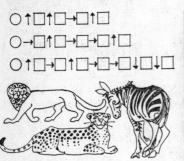

The pictures should help.

86. *April Fool joke*

In how many years during a century do Christmas Day and New Year's Day fall in the same year?

87. Riddle-me-Ree

My first is in SACK but not in SILK
My second is in HAT but not in STAND
My third is in AYE but not in OYEZ
My fourth is in KNIFE but not in FORK
My last is in FIRE but not in FLAME

What am I?

88. Word square

Can you make a word square from these clues?
  Each word has four letters.

Across and down
1. A bird is on the —
2. Just a thought.
3. Tidy.
4. This shuts in a field.

89. Riddles

The pictures are clues to help you.

1. What has legs and a back but no face?

2. Why is a whiting called a whiting?

3. What has teeth but cannot bite?

4. What has an eye but cannot see?

5. What is black and white and is read all over?

6. What is a bird after he is two days old?

7. How can you buy eggs and be sure there are no chicks in them?

8. How long will an eight-day clock go without winding?

9. What time is it when an elephant sits on the fence?

10. What word is always pronounced well?

90. Nutty sums

Tom: Did you know, Sue, 10 and 3 make 1?
Sue: No, they don't!
       Ten and three make 13
Tom: No, look at my watch.
       It's ten o'clock now.
       So in three hours' time,
       it will be . . . What?

Can you see how Tom and Sue were both right?

9 1 . Thinking straight

All dogs have four legs.
All dogs are animals.
So all animals have four legs.

Can you say if this is true or false?
Well, obviously, the last line – the conclusion – is false:
it doesn't follow from the first two sentences.
Try your reasoning skill on these sentences:
Say if the last line follows.

1. All dogs are animals.
   Lassie is a dog.
   So Lassie is an animal.  True or false?

2. All parrots are birds.
   All birds have backbones.
   Polly is a parrot.
   So Polly has a backbone.

   True or false?

3. All men are mortal (do not live for ever).
   Socrates was a man.
   So Socrates was mortal.

   True or false?

4. All penguins live at the South Pole.
   All penguins are birds.
   So all birds live at the South Pole.

   True or false?

92. Criss-crossword puzzle

The three clues will fit into the squares both ways.
Fill in the crossword.

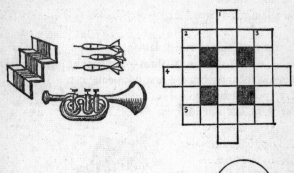

93. The Prof's picnic

Professor Brainwave took the children from his village on a picnic. The grown-ups drove them to a pretty spot beside a sunny stream. As they piled into the cars, the Professor noticed a curious mathematical fact: there were as many children in each car as there were cars altogether. When it was time to go home again, one of the cars wouldn't start. Fortunately, one of the children went home by bus and the rest crammed into the remaining cars. The Professor noticed there was one more child in each car on the way home than there had been on the way out. When they got back home, his wife asked him how many children went on the picnic. The Professor wasn't sure: 'Oh, between thirty and forty, I should say.'

'But I can work it out exactly.' And the Professor took out some empty match-boxes from a drawer he kept stocked for just such moments. 'Let these be the cars, my dear,' he said to

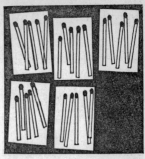

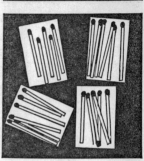

his long-suffering wife. 'Now these,' taking up some matches, 'can be the children.

'Let's say there were five cars on the way out. Now, the same number of children in each car as cars in all. That makes five children in each car. But on the way back there was one less car: that's four cars. And one boy went home by bus. So I'll remove a match. There was one more child in each car than before. That makes six in each car. And four cars in all. That gives twenty-four children. No, that's too few.'

At this point his wife swept the match-boxes off the table to lay it for supper.

How many children went to the picnic?

94. X-word puzzle

Can you solve this crossword puzzle?

If it is not your own book, don't forget to copy out the puzzle before you start writing!

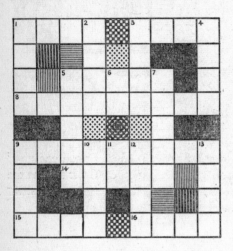

Across
  1. You plant indoor bulbs in this.
  3. A door fastener.
  5. A pompous old square.
  8. Deep, metal cooking pots.
  9. A person who collects things.
14. Wise men.
15. A wild plant growing where it is not wanted.
16. A small parasite that fastens on to the skin of dogs.

Down
  1. A narrow way over a mountain.
  2. Toilet powder.

3. To walk lamely.
4. To touch with the lips to show affection.
5. Male elephants.
6. The abbreviation for *that is.*
7. Trousers in American-English.
9. The pointed nail of a cat.
10. The fat of pigs prepared for cooking.
11. The abbreviation of *for example.*
12. A hundredth of a dollar.
13. An instrument of torture.

95. Word-building

The puzzle here is to find a single syllable or word-ending of
one word that is the beginning of another. The answer to the
first one is therefore SENT, since PRE + SENT = PRESENT
and SENT + ENCE = SENTENCE.

1. PRE — ENCE
2. FIRE — WAYS
3. PIG — TER
4. GOB — GUIST
5. BA — CERE
6. FIL — RACE
7. GLUT — IC
8. RAI — CERE
9. WOR — MENT
10. BACK — ROBE
11. MIS — TAIN
12. FRET — MILL
13. NAP — DRED
14. WEL — LY
15. HAM — TUCE

96. Caught out

What's the opposite of 'not in'?

IN   or   OUT

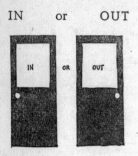

97. Tell-your-age trick

Try this one on a friend.

Say something like this to him:

'Write your shoe-size (don't bother with ½ sizes by the way).

Now multiply your shoe-size by 2 ... add 5 ... then multiply by 50. To the total, I would like you to add the Magic Number, 1722 ... and then subtract the year of your birth.

The last two figures give you your age on your birthday this year.'

Work it out with your own age first before you try it on somebody else. You'll see that it always works.

The Magic Number changes from year to year:

    In 1972 it is 1722
    In 1973 it is 1723
    In 1974 it is 1724
    In 1975 it is 1725 and so on.

98. One-stroke drawing

This interesting puzzle was invented by Lewis Carroll. Draw the three squares in one continuous line without crossing any lines or taking your pencil off the paper.

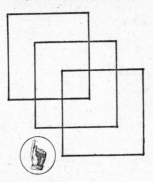

99. Puzzled ewes

Put nine sheep into four pens so that there is an odd number of sheep in each pen.

100. Manner of speaking

VE HAF VAYS OF
MAKING YOU ADMIT,
BELLOW, CHUCKLE,
DRAWL......

Here are some words to express how a person might say something: admitted, bellowed, chuckled, drawled, emphasized, fumed, gasped, harped, insisted, joked, lamented, mumbled, nattered, observed ...

These verbs of saying are often used in dialogue, like this: 'But I still think you should have warned me,' he insisted.

From the list above, which verb of saying would you choose to show that the speaker

1. was breathless with surprise
2. spoke softly and very indistinctly
3. wanted to stress what he was saying
4. was very angry indeed
5. wished to express regret
6. spoke as loudly as a bull
7. was repeating himself tiresomely
8. was speaking teasingly
9. was amused
10. was drawing out his vowel sounds

Did you notice that our list of verbs of saying was in ABC order? Can you complete our list? You should be able to complete the list except for X and Z.

101. Overworked

Abbott said Costello didn't do any work!
  This is how he worked it out.
  See if you can find the flaw in his argument.

The number of days in a year is	365 days
You sleep 8 hours a day, making in all	122 days
which leaves	243 days
You take off 52 week-ends, each 2 days	104 days in all
leaving	139 days
Three weeks' holiday is	21 days
which leaves	118 days
Easter, Whitsun, Christmas Day and Boxing Day, last another 2 days each	8 days
leaving	110 days
Six hours free every evening takes	91 to the nearest day
which leaves	19 days
Lunch hour every day takes	15 days
leaving	4 days
Two days off at the Autumn holiday leaves	2 days
Half an hour chatting-time for each of the 49 working weeks, removes another	2 days
which leaves	0 working days!

What's the catch?

102. Anagrams

A word formed from another by altering the order of the letters is called an anagram. Thus PALM is an anagram of LAMP. Can you now do the anagrams below? The first is SELDOM.

1. Make MODELS mean not often.
2. Change DEAL into a heavy metal.
3. Change MATE into a group playing together.
4. Change LIVED into a wicked spirit.
5. Change LUMP into a fruit with a stone.
6. Make READ expensive.
7. Give PEARS a very sharp point.
8. Make PORE into something to hang yourself with.
9. Make the ALPS friendly.
10. Make CANOE large and watery.

103. Paper folding

Take a big sheet of newspaper – the larger the better.
   Lay it flat, then fold it once.
   Cut it along the fold to make two separate sheets.
   Now fold, cut and stack twelve times and you get a fairly flat stack of paper.
   Just how thick do you think it will be?
   As thick as this book?
   Or as high as a table, perhaps?
   How thick?
   Guess first, then try with a sheet of newspaper and find out.

Suppose you folded, cut and stacked fifty times.
How high do you think the stack would be?

Clue: The sky's the limit!

104. Read ALL about it !

Lord Cosmic, who owns the daily newspaper the *Globe*, was boasting that he read every page of it every day. '. . . All sixty-seven pages of it, I read,' he declared.

Could he really read all sixty-seven pages of it?

(How many sides has a sheet of paper? How many sides if you fold it in two? How many if you fold it again? And so on!)

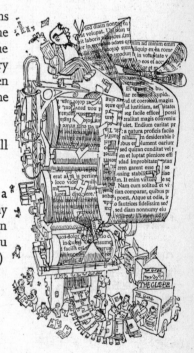

105. Paper cutting

What is the longest unbroken strip of card you can cut out of a postcard? It must be about ten centimetres wide and fifteen centimetres long.

Mr Snip tried these cuts:

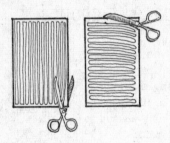

Can you get a longer strip?

It is possible to get nearly seven metres by cutting in a certain pattern. Your strips will have to be pretty thin.

106. Missing word

What's the missing word? Can you write the missing letters in the blank squares? Each three-letter column is a word and the middle row spells a well-known sea animal.

The pictures will help you.

107. Word trees

Here is a list of trees. The puzzle is to make a new word from the name of the tree by adding a single letter or group of letters chosen from the list. The letters may be added at any point in the name of the tree, but they appear in the new word in the same order as given.

Thus, by adding RER to PEACH, we get the new word PREACHER.

1.	PEACH	HET
2.	FIG	DL
3.	TEAK	U
4.	POPLAR	S
5.	YEW	ID
6.	FIR	LLO
7.	PLANE	ST
8.	PEAR	RER
9.	APPLE	T
10.	ELM	URE

108. Jim's message

Jim found this message stuffed in a bottle floating in the sea.
Can you crack the code?
Clue: The first eight words should show how to do it.

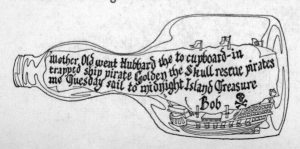

Mother Old went Hubbard the to cupboard-in
trapped ship pirate Golden the Skull rescue pirates
me Tuesday sail to midnight Island Treasure

Bob

Seeing is believing

Which of the upright lines is longer – the one on the left or the one on the right? Look, then check!

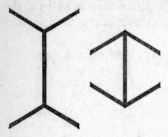

109. Kits, cats, sacks and wives

As I was going to St Ives
I met a man with seven wives.
Each wife had seven sacks,
Each sack had seven cats,
Each cat had seven kits:
Kits, cats, sacks and wives,
How many were going to St Ives?

And how many were coming away?

110. Pythagoras prohibited

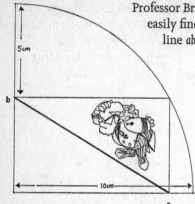

Professor Brainwave tells us you can easily find how long the slanting line *ab* is here:

'Don't use Pythagoras' theorem,' he hinted darkly. 'It's too much like hard work!

The circle's radius is 10 cm.'

111. Five-letter words

The answers to these clues are all five-letter words that begin and end with the same letter. The letter is given in brackets. To start you off, the first one is EVADE.

1. To get out of the way of (E)
2. Water flowing in a channel to the sea (R)
3. Rather fat (P)
4. To rub out (E)
5. Soft feathery stuff (F)
6. A fresh water fish (T)
7. Part of a coat or jacket (L)
8. Cleverness that enables you to do something (K)
9. Severe (H)
10. A strong sweet smell (A)

1 1 2. Rung ho !

A rope ladder hung down over the side of a ship, which was at anchor. At low tide, the Cap'n noticed that ten rungs showed above the water. At high tide, the water rose six feet above the low water level. The rungs were one foot apart. 'I wonder how many rungs will be clear of the water now?' the Cap'n wondered.

Can you tell him?

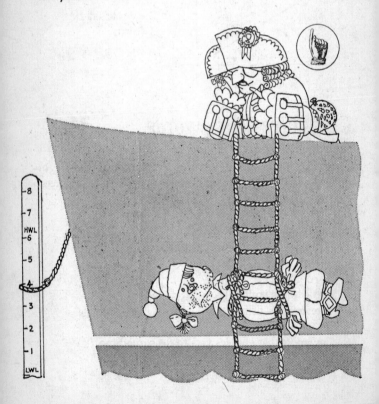

1 1 3. Triangle tangle

How many triangles are there in this figure?

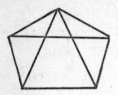

1 1 4. Fishy herring-bone pattern?

Professor Brainwave's wife bought some material to make into a suit for him, of which this is a sample. He complained that the long lines in the herring-bone pattern weren't parallel. Was he right?

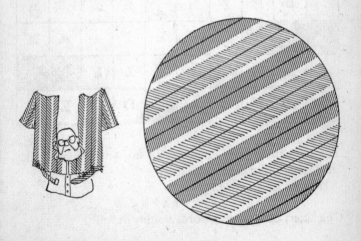

115. Muddled names

Somebody has got these well-known names muddled up.
Can you unravel them?

The Duke of Whittington
The Queen of Boots
The Wizard of Hearts
Jack and the York
Puss in Oz
Dick Seven Dwarfs
Snow White and the Beanstalk

116. Acrossword puzzle

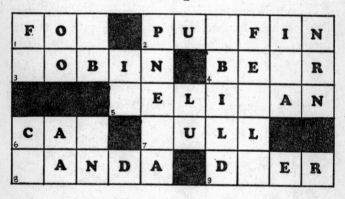

Reading across only, how quickly can you complete the
nine names of animals and birds?

Here are the missing letters:

X C P E T F A P G R

The letters do not make words reading down.

1 1 7. Words out of words

Make up as many words of three letters or more as you can, out of the letters in

BREAKFAST

Allow yourself, say, ten minutes.

Proper names are not allowed.

For example, from BREAKFAST we can get these words:

SAT, TEA, FREAK

and so on.

Remember you can count plurals made by adding the letter 's'.

Here is your rating:

85 or more	Brilliant
80	Very good
70	Good
50	Fair
45 or less	Not your day

1 1 8. Match trick

Can you make four triangles out of only six matches?

119. Xmas pud

Mrs Golightly had cooked this delicious Christmas pudding and she had slipped in the numbered coins shown:

Four children sat down to eat the pud. Could each child receive a pair of coins, hidden in his share, so that each pair adds up to the same number?

Fair and square?

Professor Brainwave decided to take the afternoon off at the fun fair. He went to the shooting gallery and this is what he saw in his gun sights. He complained that the sights were not square.

Well, are they?

Seeing is believing

Which of these circles is bigger?

Which of these shapes looks bigger?

120. What's the word?

You can make all these words from the letters of a word that names something that happens at sea.

What is the word?

wipe	hike	peck	screw	sick	rich
wiper	hire	perk	shrew	skip	ripe
wise	hip	pick	shirk	swipe	chip
wish	her	picker	ship	spike	crew
wisp	hers	pike	shriek	speck	whisker

121. Winter writing

One winter's day when it had been snowing, Ted wrote this in the snow:

Suddenly it began to snow again and the snowflakes soon covered up the letter N, which left the word 'sowing'.

For fun, Ted rubbed out another letter and again it left a word. He carried on doing this till he had only one letter and that was a word too.

How did he do it?

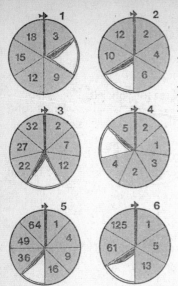

I 22.
Missing numbers

Find the missing number in each pie:

I 23. Number names

Pennie and Joe have written some numbers on the blackboard.

Can you guess their surnames?

(Hint: If not, look at the numbers in a mirror!)

Seeing is believing

Which line is longest?

Guess first, then measure and see for yourself.

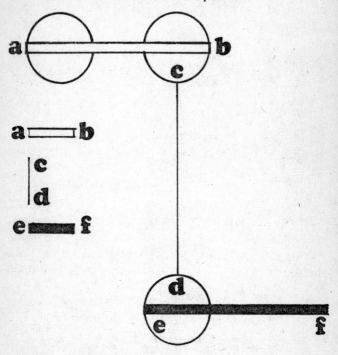

124. Groovy?

How many grooves does a gramophone record have?

Calendar trick

Here's a really puzzling trick you can play using an old calendar.

While your back is turned, ask a friend to pick a month of the calendar and draw a square round 9 dates (making a 3 by 3 square), like this:

Now ask him to add up the nine numbers inside the square. But before he does, you ask him to tell you the smallest number in the square. In this square it is 7.

Long before he has done his sums, you can tell him the sum.

This is how: add 8 to the number he gives you (7 for the square marked) and multiply the result by 9.

For example, he gives you 7 for the square above:

$$7 + 8 = 15 \qquad 15 \times 9 = 135$$

You can check that:

$$\left.\begin{array}{l} 7 + 14 + 21 \\ 8 + 15 + 22 \\ 9 + 16 + 23 \end{array}\right\} = 135$$

125. Fooled you?

How many letters are there in the alphabet?

126. Match boxes

Professor Brainwave set out thirteen matches to make six boxes all the same size and shape like this:

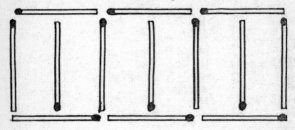

But he absent-mindedly used one to light his pipe.

'Never mind,' he said to himself, 'I can still make six boxes, all the same size and shape with the dozen matches left.'

But can you?

127. Brainwavelets

Professor Brainwave was asked how old his young children were. 'I cannot for the life of me remember. Except – wait a bit . . . If you take one age from the other, you get two; and when you multiply their ages the answer's ninety-nine. I should be able to work it out from that.'

Can you work it out before the Professor does?

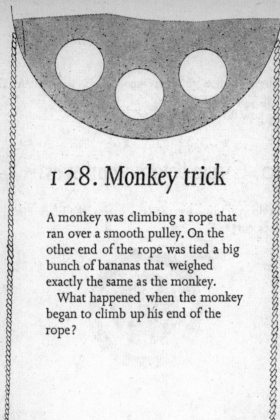

I 28. Monkey trick

A monkey was climbing a rope that ran over a smooth pulley. On the other end of the rope was tied a big bunch of bananas that weighed exactly the same as the monkey.

What happened when the monkey began to climb up his end of the rope?

1 29. Spelling bee

Say you pronounce 'gh' as in 'tough', 'o' as in 'women', and 'ti' as in 'lotion'.

Then how do you pronounce 'ghoti'?

1 30. Circle before your eyes

Which do you think has the largest area, the black circle or the black ring?

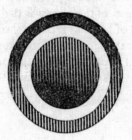

1 31. Tomato salad

Each letter stands for a different number. Can you do this sum?

```
    P O T A T O
  + T O M A T O
  ───────────────
    S A L A D S
  ───────────────
```

To start you off: the letter O means 4.

132. Beakers-and-knives

Find three empty plastic beakers and three table knives (not sharp). Stand the three beakers on the floor so they make a triangle with equal sides.

Make the distances between the beakers slightly bigger than the knives.

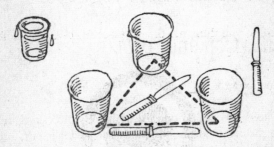

Puzzle: With the knives, make a platform on top of the beakers. No part of any knife may touch the ground. The platform must be strong enough to support a full glass of water. Turn the beakers upside down before you start.

Can you do it?

133. Thinking puzzle

Try your hand at this longer reasoning puzzle. There are three men – Jack, George and Sam.

Each has two jobs. The jobs are: driver, builder, musician, painter, gardener and hairdresser.

Can you find each man's pair of jobs from these facts:

1. The driver upset the musician by laughing at him.
   Hint: So you know the driver is not the same man as the musician.
2. Both the musician and the gardener used to go fishing with Sam.
3. The driver fell for the painter's sister.
4. Jack owed the gardener some money.
5. The painter bought paint for the builder.
6. George beat both Jack and the painter at cards.

1 34. Cop and robber

a game for two

You need two coins; one for the cop, which starts on the cop's picture; and one for the robber, which starts on the robber's picture. One player moves the 'cop' coin, the second the 'robber' coin.

The rules are simple:

1. The cop always moves first. After that, the players move in turn, from junction to junction.
2. You can move one block only, left or right, up or down.
3. The aim is for the cop to catch the robber. This is done when the cop's coin lands on top of the robber's coin.
4. The cop has to catch the robber within 25 moves. Then he wins.
5. If the robber isn't captured in 25 moves, then he wins.

There is a secret way to catch the robber. See if you can find it out by playing several games with a friend.

The city plan is on the following page.

135. The chatty taxi-rider

A lady well-known for being a talker hailed Charlie's taxi. In self-defence he pretended to be deaf and dumb: he pointed to his ears and mouth to show that he could neither hear nor speak. After reading the amount on the meter, the lady paid her fare and let herself out. Then the taxi moved off.

Suddenly the lady saw that she had been tricked.

What made her see this?

136. The odd scissors

What is so odd about the picture of these scissors?
Can you see what it is?

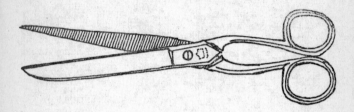

137. Tied in knots

Pull the ends of each rope shown here and three ropes will tie
themselves in knots, and two won't.

Can you pick out the two that won't?

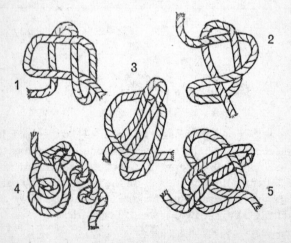

138. Triangle tart

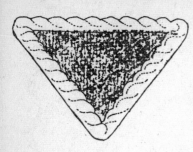

Mrs Golightly has cooked one of her delicious treacle tarts in the shape of a triangle.

She wishes to divide it between her three sons so that each gets the same amount and in the same shape.

How can she do it?

139. Awkward orchard

Can you join the trees with four lines only and without lifting your pencil?

Copy this map of an orchard and see if you can do it.

The lines must pass through each tree once only.

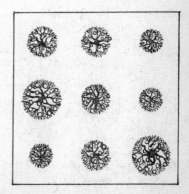

140. Möbius band

The one-twist band was invented by a German mathematician August Möbius. Actually, it only has one side.

See if you can put the jumbled lines of this limerick in the right order:

A mathematician confided
And you'll get quite a laugh
If you cut one in half
That a Möbius band is one-sided.
For it stays in one piece when divided.

141. Twisted band

Make a one-twist band but before you stick the ends of the band together, draw a line all the way down its middle on both sides. Then give it one half-twist and stick it. Take scissors and cut it right down the middle line.

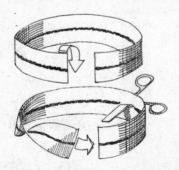

Guess how many pieces it will be cut into. Then cut it and see!

142. One-twist band

Now make a one-twist band, with a (dotted) line drawn one-third of the way across, instead of down the middle, like this:

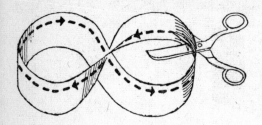

Cut along the dotted line.
How many parts does it fall into?

143. A litter of piglets

Professor Brainwave was telling his family about the litter of piglets he had seen on a farm that day.

'How many were there?' his wife asked.

'Let me see,' said the Professor. 'I remember clearly there was an odd number in the litter. And one of them was pie-bald. Two fifths of the rest were black. The rest were white . . .' At this point, the Professor's wife called him in to supper.

Can you work out how many piglets there were in the litter?

144. How many bricks

Can you tell how many bricks there are in this pile of cubes?

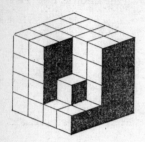

145. Spy out the spy

The map here shows four secret agents standing at street corners. A spy is hiding at one of the numbered crossings where he cannot be seen by any of the agents.

At which crossing is he hiding?

146. Kew query

At Kew Gardens, the giant Victoria lily grows in a small pond.

Suppose it doubles its size each day and it covers the whole pond – as it does – after 30 days.

After how many days does it cover half the pond?

Lightning sums

Dazzle your friends by showing them how fast you can add up.

Say to your friend:

'Jot down any two numbers you like.'

Let's say he chooses seven and four.

He writes either number below the other.

Then you say: 'Add them to get a third number. Add the third number to the one above it to get a fourth number. Carry on until you have ten numbers in a column.'

7
4
—
11
15
26

Keep your back turned while this is going on. Then turn around, draw a line under the numbers and quickly write the sum of all ten numbers.

41
67
108
175
283
—

How do you do it?

Simply note the fourth number from the bottom (here 67) and multiply it by 11. The sum is 737.

67
11
—
737

147. You have been 'ad !

Add one to seven three times and what do you get?

148. Telegraph poles

Think of a very, very long telegraph wire stretched on ten-foot poles girding the Earth's Equator.

How much longer than the Equator is the wire?

Hint: For your paper-and-pencil sums, take the Earth's radius as 4,000 miles. And pretend π is about three.

Then the Equator is $2\pi \times$ radius or $6 \times 4,000$ miles.

The Topsy Turvy name

You won't believe this, but on the blackboard here, the artist has written your name upside-down!

Just turn the page upside-down and you'll see we're right!

149. Fred's fence posts

Fred's garden fence has seven posts, each post three feet apart.

How long is his fence?

150. Tap-a-drink card

Make a card like this, with eleven holes. Ask a friend to think of one of the drinks. Turn the card over, face down.

Begin tapping the holes with a pencil. Make the first tap on the top hole. Then tap every other hole, moving clockwise. At each tap the friend spells a letter to himself.

He calls 'Stop' when the spelling is done.

Push the pencil in the last hole tapped.

Turn the card face up.

And the pencil will be in the hole by the chosen drink.

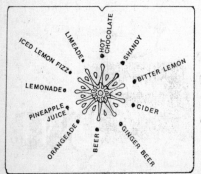

How's it done?

(Count the letters in each drink. Beer = 4.)

Sprouts

a pencil-and-paper game for two.

Begin by drawing three or four blobs anywhere on a sheet of paper.

We have drawn three:

Each player takes turns. Join any two blobs by a line – making it

as wiggly as you like so long as it doesn't cross itself – and then draw a new blob in the middle of the line:

Or you can join a blob back on to itself by a loop:

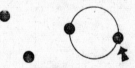

Don't forget to put a new blob on your line.
New blobs count the same as old ones.
No lines may cross:

No blob may have more than three lines going through it:

When a blob has three lines, call it 'dead' and put a stroke through it to help you see it:

The winner is the player who makes the last possible move.

Here's a sample game

Newly drawn blobs are shown in black – old ones in white.

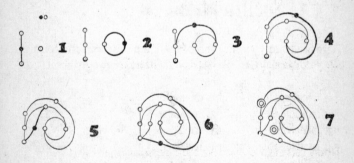

The two circled blobs ◎ have fewer than 3 lines each. But they cannot be joined because one of them is trapped!

The next player can't go. The game is won!

151. Birthday honours

You are at a party with twenty-four other youngsters. What's the chance of any of you having the same birthday?
Try it one day and you may be surprised!

152. Poles apart

A hunter set out to track a bear. He walked ten miles North, ten miles East, then ten miles South and found himself where he set out from.

What colour was the bear?

153. Spelling bee

Here are twenty words. Ten of them are misspelt, and ten are spelt correctly. Can you pick out the ten wrongly spelt?

1. innocent	11. dryness
2. innoculate	12. cosyness
3. fameous	13. truely
4. manageable	14. lovely
5. roller	15. install
6. propeler	16. untill
7. dissappear	17. forman
8. dissatisfy	18. forfeit
9. sieze	19. dynamoes
10. conceive	20. mosquitos

Answers

1 SET ARTHUR FREE

From the centre follow these numbers 6, 12, 18, 6, all numbers divisible by 6, for one way out but there are several more to find.

2. ONE-STROKE CURVES

There is a rule about such a curve. It says: you can trace it in *one stroke* only if it has two odd junctions or no odd junctions. An odd junction has an odd number of lines leading into it like these:

The one-stroke curves are: 1, 2, 4, 7, 8.

3. CYCLE PROBLEM

David is the faster: he takes seventy minutes to Sue's eighty minutes.

4. LADDERGRAPHS

1. DUST	2. LANE	3. BASK	4. BACK
DUSK	LONE	BARK	BANK
TUSK	LOSE	DARK	BANE
TASK	LOST	DART	LANE
TANK	POST	DIRT	LINE

5. ANALOGIES

1. Skin 2. right 3. more 4. wide 5. feathers 6. air
7. box 8. hair 9. often 10. bone

6. MATCHING PAIRS

1. knife and fork
2. spoon and pusher
3. cat and dog
4. oil and vinegar
5. chalk and cheese
6. house and garden
7. horse and cart
8. belt and braces
9. nut and bolt
10. pick and shovel
11. spit and polish
12. neat and tidy
13. bib and tucker
14. fife and drum
15. king and queen
16. night and day
17. sugar and spice
18. safe and sound
19. black and white
20. high and low

7. RIDDLE

Because it saw the salad dressing.

8. HIGHHAT OR BROADBRIM?

The brim is wider than the hat is tall!

9. AN ODD TRIP

Go through the town nearest to the ship and you won't have any trouble in going through an even number of towns on the way.

10. FISHY SQUARES

Eleven squares.

11. MATCHING WORDS

1. over and above
2. fair and square
3. high and dry
4. ways and means
5. brace and bit
6. pots and pans
7. safe and sound
8. part and parcel
9. tooth and nail
10. stocks and shares
11. ball and socket
12. goods and chattels
13. sackcloth and ashes
14. rack and ruin
15. bag and baggage

12. NEW YEAR BIRTHDAY HONOURS

A racehorse is automatically called a 'one-year-old' (a yearling), and its birthday is taken as 1 January – whenever it happens to be born.

13. MATCHING SOCKS

To make sure of getting a matching pair, she should take three socks.

14. WORD-DELVING

1. darn 2. coin 3. action 4. diary 5. dairy 6. yard 7. ration
8. dart 9. diction 10. irony

15. UPSIDE-DOWN

1881 and 1961.

16. TINY TIM'S JOKE

Six fives equal five sixes.

17. BEFORE YOUR VERY EYES

Actually, two circles – the smaller circle only *appears* to be bent.

18. BRAINWAVE'S EGGSAMPLE!

This is how he fenced off each egg with only three straight fences.

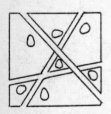

19. FIND THE VOWELS

H: Ohio	W: ewe
DH: Idaho	B: bee
Z: zoo	B: boa
G: gorilla	P: ape
RB: Arab	B: oboe
PR: opera	K: oak
CRB: caribou	R: Eire
MPRR: emperor	NN: onion
S: Asia	Y: eye
RP: Europe	SS: oasis

20. MAGIC SQUARE

All the blocks of four cells add up to thirty-four. The square is still magic when you swop the two middle-columns.

21. CONCATENATIONS!

1. con- 2. in- 3. per- 4. de- 5. ad- 6. be- 7. dis-
8. un- 9. be-

22. AS YOU WERE

Sam ended up facing the same way as the rest of the squad. You can work it out this way: a right turn and a left turn cancel each other out. So the squad – in effect – only turned left.

23. NEXT PLEASE!

22: numbers go up by 1, 2, 3, and so on.

24. SIMPLE SUM

Take I from the Roman nine, IX, and leave X or ten. Simple!

25. DOUBLE ACROSTIC

1. W	I	N	K	S	
2. A	R	R	O	W	Initial word: WASTE
3. S	W	I	N	E	Final word: SWEET

4. T	R	A	D	E
5. E	V	E	N	T

26. MORE CONCATENATIONS

1. -sist 2. -tract 3. -fer

27. BERLIN–PARIS EXPRESS

Route AEQ is the fastest.

28. REVERSE IT

12, 34, 45, 67, 78, 89 are all the other two-figure numbers that reverse when you add 9.

29. ACT ON THESE CLUES

1. DISTRACT
2. ATTRACT
3. EXACT
4. SUBTRACT
5. EXTRACT
6. COMPACT
7. PACT (or COMPACT)
8. IMPACT
9. TACT
10. TRANSACT

30. IN THE BALANCE

Four marbles balance the box.

31. WHAT'S NEXT?

The letters are the initials of: One, Two, Three, Four, Five, Six, Seven.
Next letters: E(ight), N(ine).

32. SCRAMBLED SNAP-SHOTS

a, d, e, i, c, g, b, h, f.

33. WHAT'S NEXT?

21 (= 8 + 13). Each number equals the sum of the two previous ones.

34. SPIRAL CROSSWORD

H	S	U	N	D	A	E
U	T	L	A	M	B	X
M	R	A	C	O	R	C
D	E	M	N	A	L	
R	S	E	Y	E	K	U
U		T	A	K	E	D
M	E	A	S	U	R	E

35. THE ENGLISH FAMILY ROBINSON

Bobbie and Pat have Robin as a brother: so Robin must be a man. Chris is a man. Bobbie and Pat are women because no arrow goes towards them.

36. QUICKIE

A house built at the South Pole will have all its four walls facing north.

37. A STRIKING PUZZLE!

You count the seconds *after* the first striking. That leaves five gaps between six strokes which take five seconds. After the first striking, there are eleven gaps while striking twelve. So the clock takes eleven seconds to strike twelve.

38. TAKE YOUR PARTNERS

1. broken promises
2. flat tyre
3. common sense
4. food poisoning
5. sweet tooth
6. Yorkshire pudding
7. summer holiday
8. garage mechanic
9. blind drunk
10. elbow grease
11. Catherine wheels
12. mother tongue
13. soaking wet
14. peeping Tom
15. Brazil nuts
16. plain Jane
17. howling gale
18. topsy turvy
19. tight corner
20. free enterprise

39. MIRROR

The mirror image of TIMOTHY looks the same; but BARBRA does not. The mirror image of a letter looks the same as the letter when it is symmetrical (each half is the reverse of the other, like T and O).

40. THE SECOND MAN

1. mariner: parson
2. baker: butcher
3. reporter: astronaut
4. pilot: warrior
5. lawyer: bandit
6. typist: florist
7. king: subject
8. artist: author
9. plumber: glazier
10. matron: nurse

41. BUCKET AND SPADE

The spade costs ten pence, the bucket twenty pence.

42. APRIL FOOL?

All the months have twenty-eight days! Did it fool you?

43. FROG-IN-WELL

Eight days. On the eighth day the frog climbs three metres and reaches the top of the well; he is out.

44. QUIZZLE

The word 'wrongly' is always pronounced 'wrongly'!

45. WORD SQUARE

W	I	N	E
I	D	E	A
N	E	A	R
E	A	R	N

46. PARALLEL LINES?

The horizontal lines are equal in length.

47. RIDDLE

Because the adder 'ad 'er handkerchief.

48. WORDS THAT COUNT

They are old English counting words: ane 1, tane 2, tother 3 up to gigit 20.

49. GROMEK, VERY MUCH!

Three ways: 2 Gromek, 1 Slob; 1 Gromek, 3 Slob; 5 Slob.

50. GLIDOGRAM

1.	P	H	O	E	Y
2.	S	P	H	E	R	E
3.	T	Y	P	H	U	S
4.	N	Y	M	P	H	S
5.	C	A	L	I	P	H
6.	T	R	O	P	H	Y
7.	S	I	P	H	O	N
8.	S	P	H	I	N	X
9.	P	H	R	A	S	E

51. THE SIGN

Did you say 'the' twice?
Look again and read the sign carefully. Most people overlook the second 'the'.

52. MIRROR WRITING

Sue's note says: 'Is Jennie top?'
Sally did the sum and got 40 which in a mirror reads backwards or upside down 'NO'.

53. PICTURE PUZZLE

Blackbird, butterfly, sunflower, football.

54. SEATING PROBLEMS

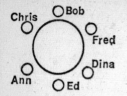

Chris	Bob
Ann	Fred
Ed	Dina

55. PUNCTUATION PUZZLES

2. That that is is. That that is not, is not. That that is not, is not that that is.

3. Jones had 'had had'. Had 'had had' been in Smith's essay, Smith had been top.

4. King Charles cracked a joke. Half an hour after, his head was cut off.

5. A window cleaner was busy cleaning. Traffic from inside the car didn't sound too loud. Cried the Major: 'Taxi!' Inside a nearby telephone kiosk, a lollipop in one hand and a plastic gun in the other, sticking his tongue out at the motorists, a small boy hung about while his aunt telephoned the Major a cab.

56. CORKING GOOD PUZZLE

Bottle costs two pence, cork one pence.

57. WHEN IS A SQUARE NOT A SQUARE?

The first is a perfect square 4·5 cm by 4·5 cm. The second is an oblong 4·5 cm by 4·1 cm.

The lower squares are identical, though the one on its point looks like a diamond and a bit larger.

58. WORD-MAKING

1. SEEP
2. SWEAR
3. PEEP
4. PEAR
5. NEAR
6. PEW
7. SEW
8. PANE
9. WREN
10. NAPE

59. RIDDLE

Because they all live there.

60. FOUR-IN-A-ROW

The children sit in this order:
Ann Bob Charles Doris

61. SUM PUZZLE

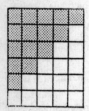

The two walls fit together like this, to form an oblong five by six bricks, making thirty bricks in all. But this is twice the number we want (because we had two walls). So the sum is half this figure, or fifteen. In the same way, the sum of the numbers from one to six is

$$\frac{6 \times 7}{2} = \frac{42}{2} = 21$$

Check this and see!

You can find out the sum of the numbers from one to as high as you like in this way, and the sum of the numbers from one to one hundred is 5050.

62. WORD STRIPS

1. NUMBER
2. DAMPER
3. WATER
4. STONE
5. BOXER

63. EXPRESS SUM

Both trains must be the same distance from London when they meet! Did you do yards of wasted sums? We warned you not to spend too long over it.

64. APRIL FOOL JOKE

You have five left. All the others are taken away.

65. HOW MANY SQUARES?

Fourteen squares – made up of nine small black and white squares, four squares (each of four small squares) and the outside frame.

66. LOONY LIMERICKS

1. There was an old Man with a nose,
   Who said, 'If you choose to suppose
       That my nose is too long,
       You are certainly wrong!'
   That remarkable Man with a nose.

2. There was a young lady of Ryde
   Who ate green apples and died:
       The apples fermented
       Inside the lamented
   And made cider inside her inside.

3. There was an Old Man of Marseilles,
   Whose daughters wore bottle-green veils;
       They caught several fish,
       Which they put in a dish,
   And sent to their Pa at Marseilles.

67. COOK TO TASTE

There are lots of obvious ways. None of them use division.

$1 + 2 + 3 + 4 + 5 + 6 + 7 + (8 \times 9)$
$- (1 \times 2) - 3 - 4 - 5 + (6 \times 7) + (8 \times 9)$
$1 + (2 \times 3) + (4 \times 5) - 6 + 7 + (8 \times 9)$
$(1 + 2 - 3 + 4) \times (- 5 + 6 + 7 + 8 + 9)$
$(- 1 - 2 + 3 - 4) \times (5 - 6 - 7 - 8 - 9)$

And some not so obvious ways:

$1 - 2 - 3 + (4 \times 5) + 67 + 8 + 9$
$1 + (2 \times 3) + 4 + 5 + 67 + 8 + 9$

$$(-1 + 2) \times (34 + 56 - 7 + 8 + 9)$$
$$1 \times 2 + 34 + 56 + 7 - 8 + 9$$
$$12 + 3 - 4 + 5 + 67 + 8 + 9$$
$$123 - 4 - 5 - 6 - 7 + 8 - 9$$
$$123 + 4 - 5 + 67 - 89$$

68. LETTER-SHUFFLING

LEFT	STEP
HORSE	CRATE
EAST	FEAT
CHEAP	READ
TEAM	EWER

69. TOPSY-TURVY YEARS

Last topsy-turvy year was 1881.

70. RIDDLE

When it is an ice-cube ball.

71. KNOTTY PROBLEM

Slip your friend's string under the string round your right wrist, to make a loop coming out the other side. Pass your right hand through this loop. Tug the string now and it should slip back through the string round your wrist. And you will be free.

72. RIDDLE

You *could* say only one bean, because then the jar would no longer be empty. But then the same thing would go for putting in, say, twenty-three beans all at once. Or you *could* say that you cannot put in any beans because the jar wouldn't be empty if you did. It's a crazy riddle!

73. STORY PAIRS

Hansel and Gretel
Peter and the Wolf
Robin Hood and Maid Marian

Jack and Jill
Tweedledee and Tweedledum
The Mad Hatter and the March Hare (It was correct all along!)

74. RIDDLE

When it is a hippopotamus baby.

75. LETTER REMOVAL

1. EASE	5. ANGER	8. CANE
2. APPLE	6. CEDAR	9. KING
3. ILL	7. PIE	10. MATURE
4. LANE		

76. BAFFLING CROSSWORD

1. B A B B L E
2. B A C H E L O R
3. B A C K W A R D
4. B A F F L E
5. B A L D
6. B A L L O T
7. B A N D Y
8. B A N Q U E T
9. B A R I T O N E
10. B A S H F U L

77. RIDDLE

When it's ajar.

78. QUICK CHANGE

1. MOANING	6. LILT
2. DRUNK	7. TROUGH
3. SEARCH	8. PATROL
4. CHARM	9. EASTERLY
5. COUGH	10. WHIMPER

79. INSIDE-OUT SENTENCES

1. The King praised the fiddlers three that brought the fiddles that made the Queen laugh.
2. We cheered the Martians that played the team that brought a Martian goat for a mascot.
3. The humming-bird has a wing that has a speed that is very fast.
4. The cow with the crumpled horn tossed the dog that worried the cat that killed the rat that ate the malt that lay in the house that Jack built.

80. POCKET-SIZE COIN

No, you can't, although the picture of the table looks quite big enough.

81. BACK-TO-FRONT WORDS

1. live, evil
2. flow, wolf
3. star, rats
4. snip, pins
5. parts, strap
6. moor, room
7. spool, loops
8. reed, deer
9. draw, ward
10. lever, revel

82. FIND THE RELATION

The man is the father of the person in the snapshot – who is his daughter.

83. SPY CODES

1. BE READY TO LEAVE AT ONCE WILLY VAN TRUBCODE BECAUSE YOU ARE BEING WATCHED
2. BE AT HOTEL BY THE OAK TREE SOON AFTER TEN BE READY TO TAKE THE TREASURE JOHNNY BREAKFAST

84. LETTER PLATE OR NUMBER PLATE?

Upside-down, it reads: LEO LION, that's why!

85. TRACKING DOWN ANIMALS

1. rhino   racoon   shark

97. TELL-YOUR-AGE TRICK

This is how it works. Say your shoe size is $6\frac{1}{2}$. You write your shoe size, ignoring the $\frac{1}{2}$ size: 6. Multiply by 2, gives 12. Add 5 gives 17. Then multiply by 50: that makes 850. To this add the Magic Number 1725 (if the year is 1975). That makes 2575. Now comes the trick. You take away the year of your birth. This is the same as the present year, 1975, less your age. That is, your birth year = 1975 − your age. So when you subtract your birth year, you are taking away 1975 and *adding* your age. Or in numbers:

$$2572 - 1975 + \text{age}$$

which equals 600 + your age. You ask only for the last two figures – which is, of course, your age. Another point is that all the adding and multiplying at the beginning is to ensure that the shoe size gets multiplied by 100. Since almost nobody's age is more than 99, you are only interested in the last two figures, so the shoe size doesn't come into the working out.

Neat, isn't it?

98. ONE-STROKE DRAWING

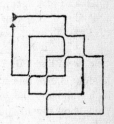

99. PUZZLED EWES

We didn't say no pen could be inside another!

100. MANNER OF SPEAKING

1. gasped
2. mumbled
3. emphasized
4. fumed
5. lamented
6. bellowed

| 7. harped | 9. chuckled |
| 8. joked | 10. drawled |

One continuation would be:

pleaded, quibbled, roared, snapped, threatened, urged, volunteered, whispered, x-, yelled, z-.

101. OVERWORKED?

The catch is simply that many of the times-off have been counted twice. For instance, the 8 hours' sleep is counted in the second line and again in the 52 week-ends, not to mention the three-weeks' holiday, Easter, Whitsun and so on.

102. ANAGRAMS

1. seldom	6. dear
2. lead	7. spear
3. team	8. rope
4. devil	9. pals
5. plum	10. ocean

103. PAPER FOLDING

Folding twelve times will make a stack about forty-one inches high – about the height of an average table.

This is how it works out.

Say newspaper is about one-hundreth of an inch thick. The thicknesses double each time, like this: 1, 2, 4, 8, 32 . . . and so on up to 4,096 for the twelfth doubling (or folding as it will be with the newspaper).

The thickness of 4,096 sheets works out at about forty-one inches or three feet five inches.

As for fifty folds, we first work out one doubled fifty times, which comes to 1,126 million million, very nearly. That is, there will be that number of sheets of newspaper, each one hundredth of an inch thick. So the stack is $1,126,000,000,000,000 \times 1/100$ inches = 170 million miles!

This is about twice as far as the Sun!!

104. READ ALL ABOUT IT!

No. Lord Cosmic's paper must have had an *even* number of pages. Work it out by folding paper. Or try to find a paper with an odd number of pages!

105. PAPER CUTTING

A spiral cut gives the longest strip:

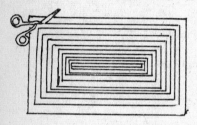

106. MISSING WORD

OYSTER

107. WORD TREES

1. PREACHER	4. POPULAR	7. PLANET	10. HELMET
2. FIGURE	5. YELLOW	8. PEDLAR	
3. STEAK	6. FIRST	9. APPLIED	

108. JIM'S MESSAGE

The first eight words are from the nursery rhyme. They show that you have to swop next-door words all the way along the message which reads:

'Old Mother Hubbard went to the cupboard – trapped in pirate ship the Golden Skull rescue me pirates sail Tuesday midnight Treasure Island Bob.'

109. KITS, CATS, SACKS AND WIVES

There was only one person going to St Ives – 'I'!
Coming away were 7 × 7 × 7 × 7 for the kits, cats, sacks and wives plus one for the man, making 2402 in all.

110. PYTHAGORAS PROHIBITED!

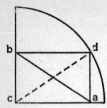

The other slant line, called *cd* here, is obviously equal to the circle's radius (10 cm). The diagonals of an oblong are equal.

So *ab* = 10 cm.

No need to use Pythagoras at all!

111. FIVE-LETTER WORDS

1. evade   6. trout
2. river   7. lapel
3. plump   8. knack
4. erase   9. harsh
5. fluff   10. aroma

112. RUNG HO!

It doesn't matter how high the water rose. The number of exposed rungs would be the same, ten, for the ship floats up with the tide.

113. TRIANGLE TANGLE

We counted eleven triangles.

114. FISHY HERRING-BONE PATTERN?

The long lines *are* parallel: they just look skew-whiff, that's all.

115. MUDDLED NAMES

The Duke of York
The Queen of Hearts
The Wizard of Oz
Jack and the Beanstalk
Puss in Boots
Dick Whittington
Snow White and the Seven Dwarfs

116. ACROSSWORD PUZZLE

1. FOX
2. PUFFIN
3. ROBIN
4. BEAR
5. PELICAN
6. CAT
7. GULL
8. PANDA
9. DEER

117. WORDS OUT OF WORDS

We managed to make one hundred words of three or more letters out of BREAKFAST

We have shown the words that can take an 's' at the end in this way -s.

are	break-s	sake
are-s	breast	sat
(units of area)	ear-s	sear
area-s	east	seat
art-s	eat-s	set
aster	fake-s	stab
ate	far	stake
baa-s	fare-s	stare
bake-s	fast	star
bar-s	faster	stark
bark-s	fat-s	steak
base	fate-s	strak
bask	fear-s	streak
basket	feast	tab-s
bast	feat-s	take-s
baste	freak-s	tar-s
baster	kart-s	tare-s
beak-s	raft-s	task
bear-s	rake-s	tea-s
beast	rat-s	teak
beat-s	rate-s	tear-s
best	rea-s	trek-s
bet-s	sabre	

133

118. MATCH TRICK

Stand them up to make a triangular pyramid (actually, a tetrahedron), like this:

The four faces make four triangles.

119. XMAS PUD

Arrange the coins in two rows and the problem becomes simplicity itself to solve:

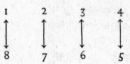

120. WHAT'S THE WORD?
The word is *shipwreck*.

121. WINTER WRITING

```
S   N   O   W   I   N   G
    S   O   W   I   N   G
        O   W   I   N   G
            W   I   N   G
            W   I   N
                I   N
                I
```

122. MISSING NUMBERS

1. 6; 2. 8; 3. 17; 4. 3; 5. 25 (they are the square numbers); 6. 29 (differences go up 4, 8, 16, 32, 64).

123. NUMBER NAMES

In a mirror, the numbers make the names: PENNIE POTS, JOE JONES

124. GROOVY?

One single groove on each side which the needle follows!

125. FOOLED YOU?

The words 'the alphabet' have eleven letters!

126. MATCH BOXES

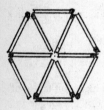

127. BRAINWAVELETS

Their ages are eleven and nine years.

128. MONKEY TRICK

This is a very old puzzle, invented by Lewis Carroll. The monkey does not get any nearer the bananas for as he climbs up the rope he hauls the bananas up at the same time. Eventually the bananas catch in the pulley.

129. SPELLING BEE

Fish

130. CIRCLE BEFORE YOUR EYES

The areas are the same!

131. TOMATO SALAD

```
345954
546954
――――――
892908
```

132. BEAKERS-AND-KNIVES

Place the glass of water on the three interlocked knives which sit on the three beakers as shown from above here:

133. THINKING PUZZLE

The best way to solve this kind of problem is to make out tables of the men and their jobs and look at the jobs that don't belong to the *same man*:

1. tells us: *driver is not musician*
2. tells us: *musician is not gardener*
3. tells us: *driver is not painter*
5. tells us: *painter is not builder*

Now for the men:

2. tells us: Sam is not musician or gardener. So put an x in the table under Sam and opposite musician and gardener.

	Jack	George	Sam
driver			
musician			x
builder			
painter			
gardener			x
hairdresser			

4. tells us: Jack is not the gardener.

	J	G	S
driver			
musician			x
builder			
painter			
gardener	x		x
hairdresser			

6. tells us George is not the painter and also Jack isn't the painter:

	J	G	S
driver			
musician			x
builder			
painter	x	x	√
gardener	x		x
hairdresser			

This gives us our first 'strike'. We now know Sam must be a painter, hence the tick. But the painter is not the builder: so an x goes in Sam's column opposite builder. Also the painter is not the driver: another x opposite driver under Sam. That leaves hairdresser for Sam's other job, so Jack and George cannot be the hairdresser, hence their x's. Now we know that George must be the gardener. So he can't be the musician.

	J	G	S
driver			x
musician		x	x
builder			x
painter	x	x	√
gardener	x	√	x
hairdresser	x	x	√

We can finish the table easily. Jack must be the musician (nobody else is) so he cannot be the driver, which leaves builder for Jack's second job.

	J	G	S
driver	x		x
musician	√	x	x
builder	√		x
painter	x	x	√
gardener	x	√	x
hairdresser	x	x	√

This leaves two blanks for George. He cannot be the builder (because Jack is) so he must be the driver.
Answer:
Jack: musician, builder
George: driver, gardener
Sam: painter, hairdresser

134. COP AND ROBBER

The way to catch the robber is this: the cop must first move to the school at the bottom left-hand corner. Once he has been round it, he is 'in step' and can catch the robber.

135. THE CHATTY TAXI-RIDER

If the driver was deaf, how could he have heard her to take her to the right place? (Well, he might have lip-read.)

136. THE ODD SCISSORS

The scissors can't close.

137. TIED IN KNOTS?

Ropes 3 and 5 will not knot – if you see what we mean.

138. TRIANGLE TART

She cuts it like this:

139. AWKWARD ORCHARD

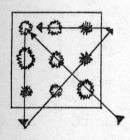

The secret is to go *outside* the orchard.

140. MÖBIUS BAND

A mathematician confided
That a Möbius band is one-sided,
And you'll get quite a laugh
If you cut one in half,
For it stays in one piece when divided.

141. TWISTED BAND

This is the famous Möbius band again: cut it down the middle and
it makes not two but *one* band – an ordinary twisted collar!

142. ONE-TWIST BAND

You get one twisted collar and one small Möbius band linked to it.

143. A LITTER OF PIGLETS

Since two fifths of the litter less one are black, the litter must be one more than a multiple of five. So it could be eleven, sixteen, twenty-one, twenty-six, thirty-one, and so on. But pigs don't usually have litters of more than eleven or so.

Check: $\frac{2}{5}$ of the litter less one $= \frac{2}{5} \times 10 = 4$.

The rest are white ($= 6$).

$6 + 4 + 1 = 11$.

144. HOW MANY BRICKS?

In a complete cube, there would be sixty-four. But eleven are missing. That leaves fifty-three in the pile.

145. SPY OUT THE SPY

The spy is standing at crossing No. 8.

146. KEW QUERY

After twenty-nine days. The next day (the thirtieth), it doubles its size and covers the whole pond.

147. YOU HAVE BEEN 'AD!

Eight – each time the same!

148. TELEGRAPH POLES

It is longer only by a mere 60 feet! Look at it this way: the wire is $2\pi \times$ (4000 miles + 10 feet) (radius of earth + height of pole), the earth is $2\pi \times$ (4000 miles), so the difference is $2\pi \times 10$ feet or 60 feet, roughly.

149. FRED'S FENCE POSTS

Eighteen feet long.

150. TAP-A-DRINK CARD

If you count the letters in each drink, name and number them off, you will find that the tappings on every other hole will work out so that four taps brings you to BEER (four letters), five taps to CIDER (five letters) and so on. (For the mathematically-minded, the trick is based on modular [or clock] arithmetic – modulo 11.)

151. BIRTHDAY HONOURS

Your chances are, mathematically, about even or fifty: fifty. More surprisingly, with fifty youngsters, you can be almost certain to find a double birthday!

152. POLES APART

Most people say the bear was white. The hunter started out from the South Pole, walked North, then East round a ring of latitude for ten miles and then back South again to the South Pole.

But there are no Polar bears at the South Pole! So we don't know what colour the bear was.

But there is a cleverer solution:

The hunter started somewhere near the North Pole, ten miles South of the latitude which is ten miles all the way round.

The hunter then walks the ten miles due North to the ring, puts a flag in the ice, then walks ten miles East until he gets back to the flag, having been all round that ring of latitude, then walks due South to his starting point. The bear was truly a white Polar bear.

153. SPELLING BEE

The wrongly spelt words spelled correctly are:

2. inoculate
3. famous
6. propeller
7. disappear
9. seize
12. cosiness
13. truly
16. until
17. foreman
19. dynamos